MW01251050

Simple Pleasures for

BUSY FAMILIES

DIMENSIONS
FOR LIVING

NASHVILLE

Simple Pleasures for Busy Families

Copyright © 1996 by Dimensions for Living

This book is printed on recycled, acid-free paper.

ISBN 0-687-05570-9

Scripture quotations noted KJV are from the King James Version of the Bible.

Those noted NIV are taken from the Holy Bible: New International Version. Copyright © 1973, 1978, 1984 by the International Bible Society. Used by permission of Zondervan Bible Publishers.

Those noted NRSV are from the New Revised Standard Version Bible, copyright © 1989 by the Division of Christian Education of the National Council of the Churches of Christ in the United States of America, and are used by permission.

That noted TLB is from *The Living Bible*, copyright © 1971 by Tyndale House Publishers, Wheaton, IL. Used by permission.

96 97 98 99 00 01 02 03 04 05—10 9 8 7 6 5 4 3 2 1

MANUFACTURED IN THE UNITED STATES OF AMERICA

You show me the path of life.
In your presence there is
fullness of joy;
in your right hand
are pleasures forevermore.

—Psalm 16:11 NRSV

One

*M*ake s'mores. Place a chocolate bar on half a graham cracker. Roast marshmallows, then place them on top of the chocolate bar. Put the other half of the graham cracker on top and enjoy.

O give thanks unto the LORD; . . . Who giveth food to all flesh: for his mercy endureth for ever.

—Psalm 136:1*a*, 25 KJV

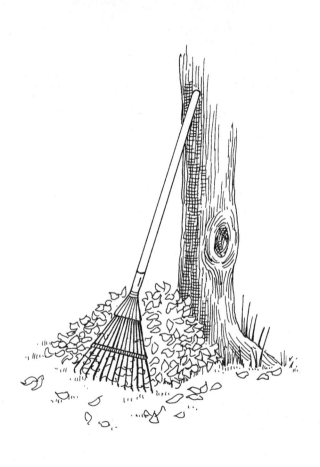

Two

*R*ake your neighbor's yard.

Each of us should please his neighbor for
his good, to build him up.

—Romans 15:2 NIV

Three

Take dog or cat food to the animal shelter.

"You are to take every kind of food that is to be eaten and store it away as food for you and for them."

—Genesis 6:21 NIV

Four

 ${\mathscr{S}}$ tart a family tradition for one weekend meal— pizza on Friday night; pancakes for Saturday breakfast; baked potatoes for Sunday night, etc.

And they continued stedfastly in the apostles' doctrine and fellowship, and in breaking of bread, and in prayers.

—Acts 2:42 KJV

Five

Have a family devotion planned by the children.

"Let the little children come to me, and do not stop them; for it is to such as these that the kingdom of heaven belongs."

—Matthew 19:13 NRSV

Six

*M*ake snow angels.

He giveth snow like wool: he scattereth the
hoarfrost like ashes.

—Psalm 147:16 KJV

Seven

Cook together as a family.

~

So they did eat, and were well filled: for he gave them their own desire.

—Psalm 78:29 KJV

Eight

*M*ake a videotape for grandparents or friends.

Yea, thou shalt see thy children's children,
and peace upon Israel.

—Psalm 128:6 KJV

Nine

$\mathcal{G}$o to the airport and watch planes take off and land.

Praise and extol and honour the King of heaven, all whose works are truth, and his ways judgment.

—Daniel 4:37 KJV

Ten

*R*ent a movie on a weekend night; then get sleeping bags and blankets, and camp out to watch it.

For I am convinced that nothing can ever separate us from His love.

—Romans 8:38 TLB

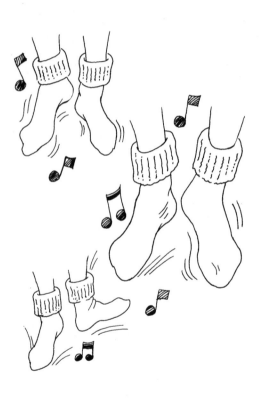

Eleven

*T*une the radio to an oldies station, take off your shoes, and have a sock hop in your house.

Let them praise his name in the dance: let them sing praises unto him with the timbrel and harp.

—Psalm 149:3 KJV

Twelve

$\mathcal{P}$ut a birdfeeder outside a window and watch what happens.

And God said, Let the waters bring forth abundantly the moving creature that hath life, and fowl that may fly above the earth in the open firmament of heaven.

—Genesis 2:20 KJV

Thirteen

Go ice skating, roller skating, or bowling.

~

A *merry heart maketh a cheerful countenance*.

—Proverbs 15:13 KJV

Fourteen

On a rainy or cold day,
spread a blanket inside
and have an indoor
picnic.

*For I have learned to be content whatever
the circumstances.*

—Philippians 4:11 NIV

Fifteen

$\mathscr{D}$esignate one night a week as family night. Let each person take turns choosing what you will do together.

Follow the way of love.

—I Corinthians 14:1 NIV

Sixteen

*R*ead a book together.
For a longer book, read a
little each night until you
finish it. Older children
can takes turns reading
aloud.

*And Philip ran thither to him, and heard him
read the prophet Esaias, and said, Under-
standest thou what thou readest?*

—Acts 8:30 KJV

Seventeen

Clean the house together. Turn on some music and dance and sing while you work.

When God gives any man wealth and possessions, and enables him to enjoy them, to accept his lot and be happy in his work—this is a gift of God.

—Ecclesiastes 5:19 NIV

Eighteen

Spend a cozy evening looking through old family photo albums. If your snapshots are all thrown in a big box, you might have several evenings of entertainment sorting and putting them into albums.

Children's children are the crown of old men;
and the glory of children are their fathers.
—Proverbs 17:6 KJV

Nineteen

*L*et one night be game night. Pop popcorn and play as many games as time will allow. Try to play each person's favorite.

So Saul said to his servants, "Provide for me someone who can play well, and bring him to me."

—I Samuel 16:17 NRSV

Twenty

$\mathscr{O}$n a sunny day, play an outdoor game together. Divide into teams if necessary, or invite another family to join you.

And the streets of the city shall be full of boys and girls playing. . . .

—Zechariah 8:5 KJV

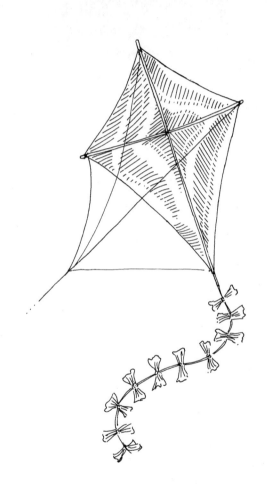

Twenty-one

Fly a kite.

The heavens declare the glory of God; and the
firmament sheweth his handiwork.

—Psalm 19:1 KJV

Twenty-two

Take a walk together and thank God for the things you see along the way.

The earth is the LORD's, and the fulness thereof; the world, and they that dwell therein.

—Psalm 24:1 KJV

Twenty-three

Go to church together.

When I remember these things, I pour out my
soul in me: for I had gone with the multitude,
I went with them to the house of God, with
the voice of joy and praise, with a multitude
that kept holyday.

—Psalm 42:4 KJV

Twenty-four

Go to a park, zoo, or museum.

And God made the beast of the earth after his
kind, and cattle after their kind, and every
thing that creepeth upon the earth after his
kind: and God saw that it was good.

—Genesis 1:25 KJV

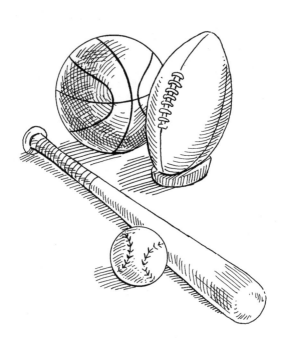

Twenty-five

*A*ttend a game of a professional team in your city or area.

Do you not know that in a race all the runners run, but only one gets the prize?

—1 Corinthians 9:24 NIV

Twenty-six

*S*pread a blanket in
your yard and watch the
clouds or count the stars.

This is the day which the LORD *hath made;*
we will rejoice and be glad in it.

—Psalm 118:24 KJV

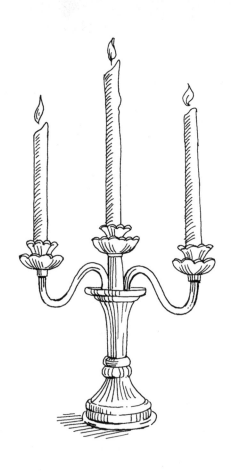

Twenty-seven

*H*ave a candlelight
dinner. Whether your
food is plain or fancy, use
your best table settings.

Thou preparest a table before me . . . ;
thou anointest my head with oil;
my cup runneth over.

—Psalm 23:5 KJV

Twenty-eight

*P*ut together a jigsaw puzzle. Leave it out on a table and work on it as you have time.

For as high as the heavens are above the earth, so great is his love for those who fear him; as far as the east is from the west, so far has he removed our transgressions from us.

—Psalm 103:11-12 NIV

Twenty-nine

Eat without utensils.

Hear, my child, your father's instruction,
and do not reject your mother's teaching;
for they are a fair garland for your head,
and pendants for your neck.

—Proverbs 1:8-9 NRSV

Thirty

Tell your all-time
favorite family stories.

A word fitly spoken is like apples of gold
in pictures of silver.

—Proverbs 25:11 KJV